Restored at last!

The Keys to Unlocking Your Restoration

Sarai Rivera-Cintrón

In loving memory of Jose I. Nazario, Jr. You will be greatly missed, but our hearts are forever imprinted with your love.

I would like to dedicate this book to two individuals who believed in me from the moment they met me: Betty Pinizzotto (foster mom), and my ESL (English as a Second Language teacher), Michele Emery.

My hope for you, my friend, is that as you read this book it brings you hope, inspiration, motivation, and that it uplifts your spirit.

Table of Contents

Acknowledgments

I would like to start out by thanking God, the One who is responsible for creating the whole universe. I thank Him for taking me through the journey of my life, and for Him never skipping a beat. All the times that I thought I was alone, He was carrying me every step of the way. I will forever be grateful to God for giving me earthly parents who brought me into this world. I want to take the time now to honor them in this book and thank them for being the best parents they knew to be due to their past hurt and pain.

I want to mention some vital individuals that God brought into my path to sharpen me in the ways of the Lord. I thank God for Rev. Gerritt Kenyon, Rev. Anita Kenyon, Rev. Wesley Kenyon, Rev. Becky Kenyon, and Rev. Esther Kenyon-Mercotte. These pastors knew me from the time I knew no English, but saw the God-given potential instilled in me and the calling God placed in my life. They brought it out of me.

I am grateful to this group of individuals whom I love as part of my family and thank God for believing in me and my calling: Dan and Betty

Mikus, Sharon Tomlin, and Juanita Nazario. I also thank God for all of you who supported me on all of my missions trips overseas from Millville First Assembly of God and Life Church in Williamstown, because you saw the calling in my life. You will all be forever a part of my family and I also dedicate this book to all of you.

I thank God for my new mentor, friend, and spiritual mom, Rev. Dr. Jamie Morgan. Thank you for always urging me to go after God and the calling He has set out before me with finesse.

I am delighted for the team who came alongside me to help me bring this book, which God called me to write, into existence. Stacey Williams, Dr. Harold Hart, and Regina Bowman, thank you for your willingness, your prayers, and your enthusiasm to make this all happen through your efforts in looking at my early manuscript, for your suggestions, and for more than anything, believing in me and this God-given project.

God knows the beginning from the end, and I thank Him for providing me with my foster mom, Betty Pinizzotto, who never gave up on me. She has been there for me through good times and bad times. She encouraged me through my high school years, college years, grad school years, and through my licensing process as a minister of the Gospel and completion through the Assemblies of God. There has never been a dull moment in our lives. Mom, I thank you for your willingness to walk side by side with me through life's journey. I want to pay you for everything you have done for me by living my life for God, regardless of what comes my way, good or bad. Without you being a part of my life, I wouldn't be who I am today, and for this, I honor you today and thank you from the bottom of my heart.

Last but not least, I want to thank my brother, Lemuel Rivera, for being there for me through the good times and the bad times. Thank you for always believing in me and for always pushing me to do the unpopular yet necessary for my growth in order to accomplish my dreams and purpose here on earth.

Judy Manalo, you have shown me what it is like to love unconditionally without expecting anything in return. Judy, I thank God for bringing you into my life. You are my gem, jewel, sister, unique, rare, and one-of-a-kind sister. I will forever love you as you have imprinted my heart with your love. Judy, I love you with all of my being.

Patience James, thank you so much for active listening, for caring, for loving me, for believing in me, and for empowering me.

I thank God for the father of my children because without him, I would not have my four treasures.

I thank God for my most precious treasures: beautiful princess, Elisabeth Maximina Huertas; and for my handsome prince, Dante Daniel Huertas. Lord, my family awaits the day when we will be able to reunite with our two babies, who were less fortunate. We love you and can't wait to meet you both in heaven some day.

As iron sharpens iron,
so one person sharpens another.
—Proverbs 27:17

Purpose of This Book

The book you hold in your hands will bring hope and inspiration into your life. It isn't by accident that you are reading this book. This day was ordained for you, and this book is a divine appointment for your restoration that awaits you. No matter what your background is, whether physical abuse, sexual abuse, emotional abuse, mental abuse, financial abuse, neglected, or abandoned, God holds the keys to your freedom from the past hurts and pains, and will bring true restoration. I dare you to try God and to put all of your past aches and pains in His hands. You won't regret it one bit.

In this book I will be sharing with you my story, my life, my pains, my disappointments, my discouragements, and how God brought true restoration into my life at last and continues to do so daily.

I welcome you to take the journey with me as I revisit my life's story, and bring encouragement, hope, inspiration, and share with you the restoration that I have received, which awaits for you to grab ahold of.

All the days ordained for me were written
in your book before one of them came to be.
    —Psalm 139:16

Chapter 1

From a Land Far Away

I was born in the hot and beautiful city of Bayamón, Puerto Rico. I lived in the amazing mountains of Barranquitas, Puerto Rico. The breeze there was always crisp. My parents' house was up on the mountains and from the outside world things seemed perfect and normal, but it was far from it. I grew up in a very dysfunctional and chaotic home, and never knew what was coming my way—whether good or bad. This was no way for a child to be brought up.

I was the youngest of my three siblings, and I can describe my childhood with one word—invisible. Things took place that should not have or that no child should have had to experience or bear, to say the least. Where was my mother through all of this? Did she have any idea of the abuse that was going on in her own home? Where was my father through all of this? Or better yet, why didn't my father protect me instead of hurting me? Why did it seem like I was the adult and my parents were the children? Why was this happening to me? Where was God through all of these horrific situations? Could an innocent child endure all that had taken place? If so, what would ever become of her? Would she ever be able to forgive? Could her broken heart ever be restored?

I grew up in a very strict Pentecostal Christian home. We went to church almost every day of the week. My birth mom loved God, the things of God, and serving in the church in many capacities. From the time I was young until I was nine years old, I witnessed my mom getting badly beat up. I also witnessed her getting verbally abused and enduring other kinds of abuse daily. I thank God for my birth mother, who taught me how to pray at an early age and also showed me the importance of combining fasting with prayer. Her dedication for the things of God made me want to know Him more and more each day. Her passion for God inspired me to do just about anything for Him. She taught me the importance of evangelizing and doing hospital visitations.

At the age of five, I handed out tracks in the city of La Vega and I learned what it was to pray for the sick to get well. I also learned what it meant to get rejected when I shared the Gospel and handed out tracks, but as a little girl, that didn't stop me. My mom is the most beautiful person, inside and out. I thank you, Mom, for teaching me the importance of remaining in God and walking close to Him daily. I also thank you, Mom, for giving birth to me regardless of the pain and suffering you were enduring through it all. I am forever indebted to you. I will always love you.

At an early age I experienced neglect, abandonment, rejection, and endured sexual, emotional, and mental abuse. As you can see, living in a very strict Pentecostal home doesn't exclude one from experiencing hardships and painful memories to have to revisit and come to terms with later on. By the time I was nine, my birth mom had endured so much abuse that she ran from it all. For years and years, I carried this with me and was angry at my mother for taking off on us. But as you continue to read this book, you will see how God turned my thinking around.

At my elementary school, I was bullied a lot from kids that knew of my mom's life. They would tell me, "I saw your new stepdad today." My mom would come to my school and ask to speak to me. She would then proceed to tell me who she was with and speak to me about things no child should have ever heard. I became the parent and she the child. I would stop her and wouldn't permit her to go on about things that were so wrong to discuss with a child. My mom's character and life choices changed dramatically. She had gone off mentally as she started struggling with mental illness. A body can only take so many beatings before the beatings start taking effect on your mind, as well as the body. The enemy was having a party with her, and pushed her so far away from the calling that God had given to her.

The next two years of my life I learned to cook, clean, and do whatever else was needed around the house, as a mother would have. My childhood years were stolen from me, as I had to meet the needs of the family as assigned to me. At this time, as you can imagine, there was a lot of discord in our home and family. God had other plans that would line us all up to be in the midst of His plan for our lives.

The LORD had said to Abram,
"Go from your country,
your people and your father's household
to the land I will show you."
—Genesis 12:1

Chapter 2

A New Journey

I came to the land of the free and many opportunities, not by choice, but I was actually abducted by my father on September 13, 1993, at the age of nine and a half. I remember being told by my biological mother years later that my father promised her, but it was more of a threat, that if she ever left him, he was going to take the kids away so that she would never see them ever again. This indeed was his way of getting revenge on her for finally having the courage to leave him because of the domestic violence and so much more.

I arrived in Millville, NJ, WadeEast projects with my father and sister. I still remember waking up from a deep sleep and saying to myself, "Where am I?" I felt like I was dropped off in the middle of nowhere, and I didn't know how to feel about the cold weather, the language being spoken, and my new surroundings. I was in a shocked state of mind.

Since it was September, this meant that it was time to enroll in school. I went to Rick Ave. I was the laughingstock of the classroom because of not knowing the language. I was picked on, made fun of, and tortured with unkind words and stares. Life, at this point, was very tough and unbearable. These barriers made things more difficult to cope with; settling in an unfamiliar place, not knowing the language, not having any friends, and not having any relatives around for the extra support.

At first, for many of my school years, I was the victim, but soon I became the bully. Why? Because hurting people hurt others, and I was one hurting soul. Even though I went to church every Sunday, I still partook in being a part of the world. I hung out with the wrong crowd, cursed, stole, and was very disrespectful to the people in higher authority. This kind of behavior landed me in the principal's office more than once.

Since I was so hurt in the past, I made sure that no one hurt me, and if someone was going to be hurt it sure was not going to be me. I dictated who I would get close to, befriend, and let in to my complicated life. I put up the walls and acted tough so that no one would get close to me. God forbid if they did; they would see that I was a hurting soul who was just waiting for someone to take the time to love on me, accept me, and believe in me.

I know what it is to move from place to place, without having any stability or consistency whatsoever. I have lived in projects, motels, and in the homes of people that I didn't even know. This kind of lifestyle took place for a good while, until a couple of incidents happened in my life that changed the path I was going on with my biological family.

"For I know the plans I have for you,"
declares the LORD, "plans to prosper you and not
to harm you, plans to give you hope and a future."
—Jeremiah 29:11

Chapter 3

Coming Out of the Cocoon

U p until the age of thirteen, I had never heard or been familiar with the term "foster care." A couple of incidents took place that landed me in the foster care system, and I became part of the state. The Division of Children and Families was going to find a foster home for me, but in the meantime I was placed with a wonderful young woman who forever changed my life and the way I view life as a whole.

I met this lady at my home church, First Assembly of God, in Millville, NJ, while I attended there with my biological family. She used to take me into her home to take me away from the chaos of my life and surroundings. I always loved going to her home, to a quiet, loving, caring, secure, and fun setting. When I couldn't go to her house, I remembered when I was last there to keep me encouraged and filled with hope.

Two weeks came and went and the phone call came in to pack my bags so that I could go to my new foster home. My foster mom, whom I now call Mom, can explain this better than I can, but for the purpose of my writing this book, I will try to explain what she shared with me years ago.

This young lady told me that when they told her to pack my bags, she saw a bright light, and she believes it was a sign from God. She said, "No, I am keeping her and her sister." To say the least, when she took us in, she was going through a divorce and hosting two other kids for the summer. She didn't have the finances to take us in and care for us. God intervened, and she obeyed His sweet, small voice and said yes to the call to care for us.

Through the years, it wasn't easy living with my foster mom. I was always afraid of being shipped off to another home, so I did my best to behave and not create any trouble that would make my fears a reality. Very little money was coming in, but I have to say, we never lacked anything. God always provided for my mom and we never, ever went hungry.

In my previous years in Puerto Rico, I never remember opening my school books to study with my biological parents. Please keep in mind that I was still struggling with the language in all of my classes in Absegami High School. My foster mom took her time, energy, and faith to believe the best in me and worked hard with me. At times when I thought I would never graduate, she would say, "Yes, you will." Lo and behold, to my own surprise, I did graduate in 1999. All of the credit goes to God and the earthly angel He placed in my life to help me get there.

I needed and craved stability; I needed and craved consistency; I needed and craved love; I needed and craved attention; and I needed and craved acceptance; and I got it all with her. This helped me grow out of my own cocoon and changed me all around, from the inside out.

I wasn't in gangs anymore, I wasn't stealing, I wasn't hanging around with the wrong crowd, and most of all, I wasn't being disrespectful to my teachers anymore. I now was seeking to help those kids that couldn't help themselves, honor those in higher authority, and love not just with my words, but also with my actions. I indeed had put the old me behind me, and brought in the new me, with God being in the center of it all.

Therefore, if anyone is in Christ,
the new creation has come:
The old has gone, the new is here!
— 2 Corinthians 5:17

Chapter 4

New Challenges

Not soon after I graduated high school, my foster mom talked about my attending college. I thought to myself, *My goodness, did you see how hard it was for me to graduate high school?* Her answer would be, "Sarai, you can do it," and the process got started to enroll. I started community college in 2001. I attended ACCC (Atlantic County Community College) in the city campus to start my general courses and then relocated to the Mays Landing, NJ, location closer to my home.

As I recall, back in those years life was tough. I had to spend countless hours reading something over and over again in order to grasp the concept of what I was reading, because I still hadn't grasped all of the basic English yet. I remember staying after class to get extra help with tutors that took the time with me to see me through my assignments. It wasn't easy, but I was determined to grasp the language, and graduate. I didn't care how long it took to accomplish this goal, as long as it got accomplished; that's all that mattered.

I was still very shy, quite, and reserved while in college. I had some acquaintances, but I didn't share much of what I had gone through or was going through. I was more or less there for them to listen to them, encourage them, and hang out with them to keep them company. I was also trying to find myself through different kinds of friendships.

Oddly enough, even though I was an introvert, I always started the conversation with the individuals who became my so-called friends. I guess I was always trying to belong somewhere to someone or to a people group. I did what they did to try to fit in, but in the midst of doing so, God would be talking to me, saying, "This is not you and you don't belong here." I thank God for always speaking to me, through His sweet, small voice, and for never giving up on me through those hard college years.

I had a couple of boyfriends, you could say, through my young college years, but none of them became serious. A couple of them wanted to marry me, and as soon as they said so, I ran the opposite direction. Sadly to say, in the relationships I had with the opposite sex, I did my best to hurt them and bring them down to nothing. Why, you might ask? Well, hurting people hurt others, and I was hurt by many male figures in my lifetime. Now that I was in control, I was the one in charge, and no one was going to hurt me again. If anything, I would be the one paying back and getting revenge for what was done to me. This type of behavior was no life, and especially not the life of a Christian lady.

A couple of years went by and I had already finished my general studies. My foster mom decided to take me to a breakaway at Valley Forge Christian College, and well, that pretty much sums it all up. While there, God took ahold of me and I knew that I needed to attend this college and finish strong. I believe that I had gone a couple of times to this college, but the last time I went was the last time for me, at least as a visitor.

It was now time to enroll at VFCC, declare a major, and get things started to attend a Christian college. For some, getting their BA done could be a piece of cake, but for me, English was my second language, so it was a very difficult task. There were so many times that I wanted to call it quits, but my foster mom was always there to remind me that quitting was not an option for me and that I was called by God to do this. Seven years later, I finally graduated with a degree in world missions and graduated from Valley Forge Christian College, now known as the University of Valley Forge.

This hard task was a major accomplishment for me. After graduating college, I then decided to go for my licensing through the Assemblies of God for preaching and proceeded to go through the long process and get licensed. I have been a licensed minister since 2008.

The education and self-growth didn't stop here. In January of 2015 I enrolled at Fordham University online MSW program, and in the fall of 2018 I graduated with honors as a master's level social worker. God always makes the impossible possible through us, but only if we allow Him to do so through the giving of our bodies as the vessels for Him to work through, and also put in the hard work and sacrifices that it requires.

I love to share my many testimonies wherever God places me to do so. I love to teach the Word and minister in any capacity that God allows me to. I let the Holy Spirit speak through me and minister through me. As I give myself to Him to allow Him to use me as His vessel, He shows up in mighty ways. I am beginning to see the many prophecies and words that have been spoken over my life years ago at work now. Why? I have allowed the power of God to heal me from the inside out. I have asked God to bring up that which doesn't belong in me and to make me more like Him, and He sure has. I want to be stripped of me daily, and be clothed with God every step of the way.

*But those who hope in the LORD will
renew their strength.
They will soar on wings like eagles;
they will run and not grow weary,
they will walk and not be faint.*
—Isaiah 40:31

Chapter 5

Soaring

I am soaring and flying at higher heights like never before. As I have given of myself to God daily with my disappointments from the past and the present, He has met me every step of the way. Years ago I asked Him to please give me unspeakable joy, and He has. How? Well, He has turned my mourning into dancing. All of the relationships with my biological family that were broken have now been restored, at last.

Months ago I took a trip to Puerto Rico, after I had a God-given dream to go there. I felt the urgency and was obedient to God to do so. I was able to relocate my birth mother and speak to her as an adult, woman to woman. I said to her, "I am here because God told me to come. I knew that He would help me find you, and He did." She looked at me with tears in her eyes and said, "I have been praying for this miracle for years." It was the best feeling in the whole entire world to look into my birth mother's eyes and tell her that I loved her and forgave her.

I told her that I loved her, but more than this, God loves her more. God wanted me to share with her about His everlasting love for her and for her to be able to grasp this truth. We hugged and kissed and hugged some more. I will never forget that beautiful day. I was filled with many emotions and feelings and I thank God I was not alone.

God was with me, and my youngest brother accompanied me on this adventurous trip. It was only three days, but we got so much more accomplished than I had ever expected because God was in it. When we do things when God tells us to, He shows up and meets us where we are at. In return, we are able to accomplish much by Him, in Him, and through Him.

I keep in contact with my birth mother, Dorys, through either phone calls or by writing letters, as time permits it, and as we are able to reach out to each other. I might not see her every day, but I thank God for her and pray for her like never before. I love her and I thank God for selecting her to be my mom. Instead of focusing on all the bad things that went wrong with my mom and me, I choose to focus on all of the things that went right and all of the things she taught me as a child until the age of nine. I learned of so many similarities we share when I went on a quest to find her. I love this woman and I am so proud to call her my birth mother. Without her, I wouldn't be here today. Indeed, this mother-daughter relationship has been restored at last.

The relationship with my father has always been one of long distance. I tried bringing him together with my kids, but many times, the past came to haunt or hurt me. I then went three steps back instead of forward. There were times when I just wrote him or texted him when God told me to. There were other times when I wanted nothing to do with him and couldn't care less if we restored the father-daughter relationship again. Truth be told, deep inside I really wanted to make things right with my father and be able to connect with him again and unite him with his grandkids. As you can see, there were some things that were easier than others, but through it all I listened to God. Sometimes I was stubborn, hardheaded, or just wanted to give up, but giving up is not in God's vocabulary.

I kept on giving of myself to God and saying, "Here I am again, Lord. Please take it all. I surrender all. Please help me forget the bad times and only remember the good times." I have to say that God has been so faithful to me and has allowed me to forget many things. The truth is that my dad isn't getting any younger, and God has changed my thinking into this: God wants me to love my father and forgive him. Love covers a multitude of sins, and God shared with me that this is what's going to bring a lot of healing to him and me. *Forgiving* is a key factor for receiving restoration at last.

For the past year, I haven't seen my dad and have been communicating via calls, texts, or mail, but today was a different kind of a Sunday. Saturday, March 15, 2014, I asked my six-year-old son, "Would you like to go visit Pop Pop tomorrow?" and he said, "Oh yes, Mommy, I love him." My father lived nearby and I knew that God wanted me to go and spend quality time with the kids and him. March 16, 2014, I took my kids to see their Pop Pop and we had a great time. I ordered pizza for us and treated us all to a quick, easy, not messy dinner.

At first I felt a bit nervous, because the mind has a way of being triggered and memories from the past came rushing back out of nowhere, but as time went on I made it through. The last time my father saw Elisabeth was when she was a baby, and now she was walking and talking some. He was talking with her and kept saying Pop Pop to her and soon she said it herself, "Pop Pop."

I could tell that day was a phenomenal day for my dad and perhaps an answer to prayer for him and me. This father-daughter relationship had been restored at last. I came home and all I could do was cry and thank God for giving me the breakthrough I needed for years and finally experienced that day. I will never be the same.

That day marked an important day in my life. As I go through life's journey now, I know deep in my heart that I have forgiven those who hurt me deeply, including my father. This, in essence, is an important key to receiving your ultimate restoration. I now keep a long-distance relationship with my father, because after all, sometimes this is the best that can be done in order to utilize wisdom so that history doesn't repeat itself.

It is very important to keep in mind that if an individual has not changed their old ways, or showed you that they have not taken the necessary steps to get some healing themselves and change for the better, then this is when wisdom kicks in and you love and pray from afar. You can forgive, but unfortunately, sometimes the other person might be hit with the consequences they brought to themselves, until trust is rebuilt again and dramatic changes are seen at a distance.

In order to keep someone from the past in your life that has caused suffering and pain, the other person must show you in more than one way that they aren't just saying that they are going to change but that there are actions behind their words in the present. If not, their words are dead, and you must remove them from your inner circle and love and pray from afar.

The purpose for this book is to bring honor to my parents and my godly foster mom, and to encourage you, to inspire you, and to challenge you to take the journey of finally being restored from whatever you have been dealing with for years. It is never too late to surrender all to God and let Him do heart surgery in you. This is one of the best seasons you will ever be in and come out of victoriously. Don't you want to soar high instead of being weighed down with anger, turmoil, bitterness, and hate?

I am sure names kept popping in your head or you saw people's faces as you were reading my life story. God is calling you to take the challenge to be restored at last. Will you take the challenge? Will you seek to be restored at last, or will you stay broken for the rest of your life? The choice is yours. Remember that you will not be able to soar high unless you allow God to restore you and make you light so that you can go to higher heights in Him and be restored at last.

Love is patient, love is kind. It does not envy, it does not boast, it is not proud. It is not rude, it is not self-seeking, it is not easily angered, it keeps no record of wrongs. Love does not delight in evil but rejoices with the truth. It always protects, always trusts, always hopes, always perseveres. Love never fails.
—1 Corinthians 13:4-8

Chapter 6

New Beginnings

I am so happy to share with you that God has done so much restoration in my life. The restoration didn't stop with my family, but it continued with my marriage. The first years of my marriage were trying ones, due to the fact that I brought a lot of baggage from the past with me into the marriage. The first year I was ready to leave the marriage any time we got into an argument, because that was the usual pattern in the previous relationships I had been in. This time it was a different story because I was married and had a newborn to deal with. I contemplated divorce many times, but it wasn't an option for either of us. We both came from divorced parents and were devoted to see this marriage through anything.

Because of all the traumatic things I saw and endured in my childhood years, I had brought a lot of baggage into my marriage. I was very insecure, jealous, unforgiving, bitter, and the list goes on. My husband stuck with me through these hard times and showed me that regardless of how I treated him, he was going to remain with me through the good times and the bad times.

There were times in the marriage where I took my anger out on my husband and I was physically abusive towards him, because he tried to hold me down as I told him to leave me alone when we would get into arguments. Afterwards I felt so bad and guilty for treating my husband in such a way. God would remind me again and again that I was to treat him with care and build him up—not tear him down. But as you can see, this was very difficult for me when I would ask to be left alone but my wishes were not respected or honored.

I continued to put myself at the Potter's wheel and asked God to reshape the parts of me that were marred. It was a very slow process, but my husband stuck by me and continued to encourage me in the Lord. A couple of years passed and I stopped being physically abusive with my husband, when we would get into arguments. But then it went from hitting to tearing him down verbally.

It is very difficult to keep it together when you are already mad, you are asking to be left alone, and your wishes are not being heard, respected, or honored. I am ashamed to say this, but we said things to each other that I never wished I had said to him or wished that I had heard from him. I was one hurting soul who happened to be angry from the past pain and was angry with the present pain that my marriage was under.

Through all of the rough years, I thank God for giving my loved ones the patience, endurance, and perseverance to see me through these hard times. They prayed me through, encouraged me, challenged me, but most of all loved me, regardless of what I went through. *Love* was a key factor in my healing process. Another key factor was being able to *trust* them and not bring the lack of trust into the picture because of how I was betrayed by the people I trusted when I was a child, and not blame them for my past pains and hurts.

If you are the one that has been hurt and taken advantage of, hope and restoration await you. If you are the one who administered the hurt and took advantage of someone's innocence, hope and restoration await you. If you are the one in the relationship waiting for the restoration to take place, please keep on keeping on praying your mate through. Don't give up on them, and continue to love them regardless of their responses towards you. Love at all costs, and know that your rewards will be waiting for you as you stay faithful to God and to your mate. I am so thrilled to share with you that what the enemy intended for evil, God has used for His glory and honor.

I spent many years of my marriage running away from my husband when it came time to be intimate. All of the past experiences left me not wanting to be intimate with him, because that triggered the many times I was sexually abused. Through these times, my husband waited for me, prayed for me, held me, and just comforted me. Seven years later into our marriage, I enjoy being with my husband and welcome intimate moments, because God healed my memory of the awful memories and I am now making new memories with my husband. I am enjoying marriage the way God intended it to be enjoyed. The enemy can't have my marriage. I have taken my marriage back, and now our relationship is better than it has ever been. Whether you are that husband that was abused or the wife who has been sexually abused, or can identify with my life story because you have been through it yourself, there is hope and restoration for you, your relationships, and your marriage. I am living proof for you.

Marriage is not easy. It is a daily choice to keep on fighting the good fight with God on our side. But with God, all things are possible. Another key factor in being fully restored at last is *knowing*

Jesus as your Lord and Savior and accepting Him into your life. His everlasting, unending love will change you from glory to glory.

As I am writing this book, God is bringing to mind that another key factor to being restored at last is *opening up* to your trusted mate about the hurting things that happened in your past. If you have been emotionally, physically, and sexually abused in the past, have you shared this experience or experiences with your mate, besides your counselor or a trusted one?

If the answer is no, choosing wisdom at all cost, ask God to help you discern who you can open up to, and with that comes healing, because the truth shall set you free indeed. I urge you again to ask God and utilize wisdom even if it is your mate. Unfortunately, I learned the hard way that very sensitive information I shared with my mate was then used against me when he was mad at me. This kind of treatment is very hard to go through as well. Therefore, I am warning you of this before you open up to the wrong person—yes, that sometimes includes your mate.

I have and continue to keep myself at the Potter's wheel. I have done counseling by myself and have also done marriage counseling, to get to where I am today. *Counseling* is another key element into receiving restoration at last. Don't you ever be ashamed for receiving counseling. Going to counseling allowed me to open up about everything, come to terms with everything, and obtain new coping skills to deal with the past, the present, and the future.

Here is another key factor about receiving restoration at last. If you attend a church where they have a *deliverance ministry team* to receive deliverance prayer, I highly recommend this. If you don't, I recommend you get in contact with a church that has this ministry. This is very vital to your whole being. This is something that can be done throughout your lifetime of being restored at last, as this is a daily process in the journey that we call life.

It takes a desire and work to make the abnormal, which was the norm, become normal again. Since my childhood was filled with a lot of chaos and I saw a lot, I was always suspicious of having a quiet atmosphere because this was not the norm for me when I was growing up. I now welcome those peaceful moments and try to keep them a part of our daily living, instead of a hostile atmosphere. I am a restored one because God has taken the cracks from the vessel and reshaped them into a new vessel without any cracks. I love my life, I love my family, and I love my marriage. I am whole and restored at last.

And they have conquered him by the blood of the Lamb and by the word of their testimony, for they loved not their lives even unto death.
Revelation 12:11, ESV

Chapter 7

Unveiling the Truth

As a child and all the way up until before marriage, I told myself over and over again that I would not let history repeat itself with what I saw my birth mother endure through her marriage. I also told myself that I would never in a million years go through a divorce. Well, I found out that I spoke too soon. In this chapter I plan to unveil to you the truth about my marriage—yes, the truth I never told the world. Another key factor to receiving restoration at last is to be *honest with yourself and others* about what is really happening in order to bring the truth to light.

As I read this book again to work on my last chapter I realized that I only focused on me and not also on my mate when I was referring to "our" marriage. I have come to the conclusion now that when two people come together in a marriage, they both bring baggage into the relationship; two people are imperfect, two people should be devoted to making the relationship work, two people should not only do counseling individually but also as a couple who both want the therapy — not just a one-sided deal.

I realized that me wanting to work on the marriage was a one-sided thing, one that couldn't save the marriage. In order to have a marriage work the two individuals must not just say they want to make it work, but their actions should prove that statement instantly. Talk is cheap but actions are priceless.

When you are stuck in a marriage where you hear over and over again that you are crazy, that you are the problem, that you are the one with all of the issues, and that you are the reason why the marriage isn't working well, you start believing it as you are gradually being brainwashed. I was brainwashed but I now know the truth and the truth shall set me free.

I was pregnant out of wedlock, and soon after I decided to marry the father of my unborn child. I thought I knew this person. He said he was a Christian. I thought he was a Christian. I believed him without taking the time to inspect the fruits and character of a true Christian. I thought I was in love. I thought he was the one. I thought he had no baggage or childhood trauma but he did, and I didn't truly know the effects that come with that and the extra work required to make a marriage work with childhood trauma from both parties.

I was just in denial and so was he. He was in denial that any of his traumatic past happened and that he needed to work through it so that it didn't affect our marriage. The denial was real from both sides. Another important key factor to receiving true restoration at last is *facing the truth head-on* and seeing it for what it is. That is indeed winning half of the battle. One skewed perspective can destroy a marriage, due to a childhood trauma and familiar experiences.

Looking back now I see all of the red flags that I should have ended the relationship. Actually while we were dating I tried breaking up four times, but it never prevailed. The truth was that he was broken and so was I. The reality was these two broken people coming together for the sake of a child and our Christian reputation because we were pregnant out of wedlock was perhaps not a reason for us or me to get married.

I told myself that I wouldn't be subjected to a relationship where domestic violence was present. Well, I was wrong. The first year there was domestic violence going on. As we discussed and argued I would make the conscious and wise decision to walk away but I quickly was followed, and held down against my will.

As the years progressed in my marriage I continued to allow the behavior to continue and things escalated for the worse. I started getting more and more afraid for my life as the behavior of my husband became worse. It is hard to tell someone that they have an anger issue to work on, when pride is so prevalent. How do you tell a prideful person that they have issues? How do you tell a prideful person that their pride and denial is what is breaking the marriage apart? How do you tell a prideful person that because of their lack of empathy, honesty, respect, and domestic violence the marriage can't go on?

I prayed, I fasted, I sought out pastoral help, I sought out counseling help, but at the end of the day it needed to be more than just me wanting the help. Many times I told my husband to please calm himself down and not lose it while our children were around but he wasn't able to calm his bad temper. As the years went by our children were getting used to the arguing, the fights, and our poor children were suffering because of it. As parents we weren't giving our children the healthy environment that is necessary to thrive, have a great quality of life, and well-being.

After many years of different events that took place, and me talking things out with a few trusted individuals who had my back and encouraged me not to take this type of behavior any longer, I decided that enough was enough. I decided that I would end this ugly and scary cycle of domestic violence abuse and that I would put an end to it once and for all on June 18, 2019. I will spare you all the details and will say that after the scary event that took place on this day, I decided to not only get a restraining order but to also start a complaint for a divorce. I had enough of being subject to mental abuse, emotional abuse, physical abuse, and financial abuse.

It is amazing to believe that in the body of Christ, people holding titles as pastors, etc., are the abusers in a domestic violence case as well. Many times as we open up about domestic violence in general or in the Church body, people don't know how to deal with it or perhaps many times we aren't believed, but that is no way for a human being to live.

I choose to give my children the very best regardless of what some of the Christian circles might tell me about divorce or look down on me for. I don't believe in divorce; however, if you are in a domestic violence case that gets worse before it gets better, get the heck out as fast as you can. God is love and God doesn't like His people being hurt through domestic violence. Your children's life and yours depend on it.

I am proud to say that I stuck by my husband until I couldn't do it anymore. I continue to pray for my soon-to-be ex-husband, so that he can surrender his heart to God in order for God to truly do the mighty work from the inside out. I will forever remain thankful to him for our children whom I adore and who will always be my treasure here on earth.

Divorce is an ugly word in the Christian world; however, sometimes divorce is necessary. I know it was in my case. A few key elements to restoration at last with divorce in mind, whether you are contemplating it, going through it, or have gone through it, is *getting rid of anger, bitterness, and revenge.* God is your vindicator and God is a just God. As you let go of these key elements your restoration will be a sweet one filled with forgiveness, love, and peace for that person that hurt you the most.

I know that as I go through the process of divorce I will continue to stay at the Potter's wheel so that I can have more of Him in me and less of me and that I can continue to receive restoration at last, through this life-changing event.

The last key factor to obtaining and keeping restoration at last is to *pray for those who have wronged you, hurt you, and betrayed you.* This important key factor will keep you grounded and away from having bitterness and resentment towards the person or persons who have hurt you in the past or present.

I pray that as you go through your journey of restoration at last that you don't give up on yourself because God hasn't and neither have I. God and I believe in your true restoration at last.

I sincerely thank you from the bottom of my heart for spending your quality time reading my life story of how God has restored me at last and how God can do the very same for you. God continues to restore me at last from glory to glory.

Will you join the restoration at last movement? Come aboard and enjoy the process of the journey. One journey that you don't walk alone, but that God is in it every step of the way.

As you go through life, life will happen and there will be speed bumps on your journey that will cause you to get back up again at the Potter's wheel so that He can continue to bring restoration at last from glory to glory. The best way to live life so that God can continue to keep you restored over and over again is to stay at the Potter's wheel and never slip off of it. Restoration is an ongoing process as you journey through life, every step of the way.

Now it's your turn to be restored at last! I dare you to put the different things you read into existence in your life, family, marriage, and/or if you are divorced. Your life, family, and marriage will never be the same. Restoration is calling you and saying, "Try me." You will not regret it because your reward will be restoration at last.

I can do all this through him
who gives me strength.
—Philippians 4:13

Closing Remarks

Thank you for taking the time to read this book about my life. I pray that it has been a blessing to you and that it has given you the courage to do what God has been calling you to do for years, months, days, hours, minutes, and seconds. The reward is so much better than the pain you have gone through. God is able and ready to meet you where you are at. Take courage and just do it for God. God doesn't expect you to do this alone. He will carry you every step of the way. All you have to do is surrender so that your reward can also be restoration at last. I urge you to not only take this challenge of being restored at last, but also ask God to show you who you can bless with this book so that they can also take the same challenge and receive total restoration at last.

Dear God ,

I thank You for the beloved one who is holding this book at this time. I thank You for compelling them to pick up this book, read it, persevere, and take the challenge to be restored at last. I thank You in advance for restoring relationships, for bringing hope to the hopeless, and for bringing healing in body, mind, and spirit to the reader. I thank You in advance for the wonderful rewards You are going to bless them with as they are obedient to Your sweet, small voice. Thank You, God, for Your Holy Spirit revealing Himself to the readers and encountering each one of them every step of the way. In the mighty name of Jesus I pray. Amen.

LOVE

You desire it, so you chase after it.
You chase after it, in the wrong places.
You catch it, but not for long because it is a
counterfeit kind of love.
The kind of love that leaves you empty,
wanting more.
That is, until you try this kind of love.
This kind of love is like no other.
This kind of love is real.
Yes, this kind of love is unconditional.
This kind of love will fill you up, and overflow.
This kind of love can only be found in God.
This kind of love will reside inside of you, once
you say YES to God.
What's love got to do with it?
Love has everything to do with it.
Now that you have this kind of love, there is no
more desiring or chasing after counterfeits.
Why?
Because you have now found the ultimate kind
of love—God.

Breathed by the Holy Spirit
Written by Sarai Huertas

Contact Information

Please feel free to contact me via email, YouTube, Facebook, or LinkedIn listed below. Let me know how this book has been of help to you, encouraged you, and/or inspired you to have taken the restored at last challenge. Should you want to book me to speak at an event of yours, please don't hesitate to contact me and I will be more than happy to make this happen. I am here at your service, serving one soul at a time, ready and willing to be a blessing to you and yours. God bless!

Email Account: RestoredAtLast1@gmail.com
YouTube: Sarai Rivera-Cintrón
LinkedIn: Sarai Rivera-Cintrón
Facebook: Sarai Rivera-Cintrón

About the Author

I was born and raised in Barranquitas, Puerto Rico, and have lived in the United States since 1993. I obtained my bachelor's degree in world missions through the University of Valley Forge. I was married in 2007, and the best gift that came out of that is my two beautiful children: our daughter, Elisabeth Maximina, and our son, Dante Daniel, and two in heaven. I received my license from the Assemblies of God in 2008 and my master's degree in social work through Fordham University in 2018. I was an AG licensed minister for twelve years. I look forward to growing as a social worker and continuing this journey of social work. I always enjoy sharing my testimony and preaching the good news to everyone who gives me the opportunity to do so. My mission field is wherever I go. My passion is serving God by serving people. I will take my social work and ministry skills to further God's Kingdom for His glory and honor everywhere I go to the ends of the world until the day I take my last breath.

Made in the USA
Middletown, DE
11 October 2020